Interviews and Interrogations

Investigative Process and Standards

A systematic approach to gathering information and getting confessions.

Death Investigation Training Academy™

ditacademy.org

ISBN:1530372682
ISBN-13:9781530372683

DEDICATION

To all investigators of death. Your job is highly respected yet under appreciated. Your dedication to improvement is honoring. It has been said, and I believe the quote. “To the living we owe respect and to the dead we owe the truth.”

“People are destroyed for lack of knowledge”
Hosea 4:6

Table of Contents

ACKNOWLEDGMENTS

This book is part of a training program of the Death Investigation Training Academy™ – a Missouri company. More information can be found at:
ditacademy.org

1. Defining Interviews

An interview is a non-accusatory question and answer session with a suspect, victim or witness. The goal of an interview is to gather information and make an assessment of the subject's credibility.

An interview at its basic level is a conversation with people associated, or believed to be associated, with your case to gather information relevant to your case. These are not interrogations so no Miranda warnings are necessary.

An interview could turn into an interrogation if certain statements are made, or your mind set changes concerning the person to whom you are speaking.

It is important to remember that ***witnesses lie***. They do not always lie on purpose however. Just because a person feels positive about what they are saying does not mean they are accurate.

Three critical areas affect how a person's statement is impacted.

1. Memory
2. Perception
3. Bias and Prejudices

2. Cognitive Psychology

An investigator must have an understanding of how the memory works and why things like trauma, stress, and fear can play a role in memory. The aim of cognitive questioning is to mentally reinstate the context of an incident in order to better retrieve details from memory.

A cooperative witness will desire to tell what they remember. However, they might not have a full narrative without some distortion. Distortion can be caused from one of the three areas that effect memory, or simply what they believe they saw.

For instance, depending on the direction of the sun, the color of a vehicle, and a persons ability to see color, the witness may fully believe the car they saw was blue. However, witnesses from the opposite side of the street may say the car was green. Both may be telling you the truth as they saw it.

Caution: Do not ever feed or plant information or ideas. If a witness says the car was blue then take that statement, never ask them if they are sure because others have said it was green. By doing this you have further distorted the statement and, in fact, this witness may be correct or at least the most honest.

This is the same reason we separate witnesses as soon as possible. First, so that "stories" cannot be formed, and secondly so that crowd mentality will not change another person's honest feelings. People do not like to be the only one with a different answer, they will many times feel they must be wrong and others are right. You may then lose the only real information you would have gotten.

Investigators need to use caution in the area of "trusting your gut". It is true that the longer you work in the field of law enforcement, you will eventually begin to develop a sense of things, known as the sixth sense. Whereas this can be beneficial in cases of safety, it should not be used in interviewing.

An interviewer must talk with witnesses without any bias or predetermination. Doing so can shape your investigation even without you being fully aware of it. Never "claim" a suspect and then find the evidence to prove your case.

Witnesses can be vulnerable and you may inadvertently mislead them. This can result in a bad case law, no conviction, and embarrassment for you and your agency. Worse yet, it could result in the conviction of an innocent person and subsequent personal and professional lawsuits.

Cognitive Questioning

Begin with open ended questions which urge the witness to recall everything in chronological order. Starting with a physical description of the environment; ask about sounds, smells, tastes, and feeling.

Allow the witness to recount the incident as fully as possible without interruption. Then ask the witness to change perspectives and re-describe the incident. Ask them to explain as if they were in another vantage point or ask them to recount the incident from the suspect's perspective. These may not always be accurate but it aids in them recalling details they may have otherwise forgotten. Next, have them start their explanation again from their first and primary vantage point, telling the story from a certain point in the story you choose; such as "right after you heard the gun go off" or "starting from the time you entered the room", have them tell the story in chronological order from there.

Reverse order recall

Another helpful tool in cognitive questioning is to get the person to recall the incident in reverse order, for example. *From the time you arrived here in the hospital, tell me everything that happened before that. Just go back over everything in reverse - what happened before that, what happened before that, and so on.*

3. Interviewing a Witness

Witnesses are people with information; information you want. These may be witnesses at the scene, a co-worker, employers, a person suggested by another witness, or those contacted during an area canvass.

Keep in mind that you could stumble upon and interview the suspect without initially knowing it. Suspects like to be considered a witness; this keeps them "in the know" and keeps the heat off of them.

Proper approach and attitude are very important when dealing with witnesses. You have to be the nice guy. The people you are talking to may want to protect their friend or family member. It is possible as well that they truly have no information about the case. It is also very possible that these people are in fear of telling you what they know.

When you first make contact and after introducing yourself and explaining why you are speaking to them, get all contact information – **Be sure you can find them later**!

- Full name including nicknames and street names
- Gang affiliations
- Address and Phone Number including house and cell (verify cell while there – call it)
- Email address
- Employer – name and address
- Occupation in case they change employers
- Closest relative name and contact information

After you have gathered all the information you can to assist you in finding them later, get an initial statement. Let them tell you their version of events, even if you think or know it's a lie. Let them tell it their way do not correct them. Get them to give you a written statement whenever possible. Remember, **witnesses lie** and that's okay. Continue to build your case and the ones you later find have lied are your best re-interviews. Re-interviews can produce valuable information when you can prove their first statement was a lie. The interviewee may be more cooperative after facing possible charges of giving false information or interference with law enforcement." Document what they say in your notes and, once again, get them put their statement in writing."

Audio – Video Statements

In some cases it is feasible to get statements on audio and/or video. Be sure to check your state law concerning covert audio. In Missouri, a conversation can be audio recorded as long as at least one of the persons involved in the conversation knows its being recorded. It is not necessary for the witness to know. However, Washington State for example is a two-party consent state. Both parties must consent to recording.

Body cameras are great tools to record witness statements. The laws allow for police interactions to be recorded through either in car dash-cams or uniform affixed body cameras. This makes great evidence of statements during an interview.

Overcoming the biggest obstacle

A big obstacle to overcome is the "I do not want to get involved" statement. This can be extremely hard to overcome due to fear or complacency of the witness. You can at times attempt to overcome this with reason formulation, ie. (playing on the common good for the community, victim, etc.) In some cases, you can use the threat of hindering prosecution or interfering with a police investigation charge. Use caution before making this threat. You need to be fully ready and authorized to make this arrest and this tactic should only be used after all other attempts have failed. You should not use this intimidation tactic and then not follow through. Further, you cannot make this threat if you do not have the legal standing to follow through or the backing of your agency and/or prosecuting attorney.

If you fail to get cooperation, thank them for their time and explain you will be in touch at a later date. Never let them think its over, even if it is. This keeps them on edge and they may contact you later themselves.

4. Interviewing Family Members

An investigator's approach to family members must be one of total respect and understanding. Your approach and attitude must be above normal standards in these types of interviews. Your attitude and demeanor upon first contact will set the tone for the rest of the conversation. This includes the officers that arrived on the scene first. If you have to talk with family or even witnesses, hours or days later, you can be sure the attitude of the officers on the scene during the initial call will be a factor in the cooperation you will get today.

Find your empathetic side. Keep in mind the information these family members give might send their loved one to prison. You are going to have to gain their trust, and show concern and empathy to these people. But also keep in mind that **family will sometimes lie!**

As pointed out in chapter 3, when you first make contact and after introducing yourself and explaining why you are speaking to them, get all contact information – **Be sure you can find them later**!

- Full name including nicknames and street names
- Gang affiliations
- Address and phone number including house and cell (verify cell while there – call it)
- Email address
- Employer – name and address
- Occupation in case they change employers
- Closest relative name and contact information

After you have gathered all contact information, ask your questions in an organized manner and let them tell you their story their way. Do not interrupt or correct at this point. Once they are done you can go back and use the cognitive interview approach discussed earlier and achieve more clarity to their statements

Be sure to get something before you leave. Their hand written statement is best, but at the very least be sure you have taken good notes during the cognitive questioning process.

Interviewing family of a decedent

If you are talking with a family member of a decedent, be sympathetic to their situation. Be real, this could be you someday. When possible, have them sit down. The kitchen table is best if available, create a relaxed non-threatening environment. Never use police jargon or talk "police speak" - talk to them like a normal person.

If talking about a deceased family member, never refer to the dead as "the deceased" or "the body". Call the deceased by their name. Offer support to the person you are talking to but be careful never to say things like:

- I know how you feel – (no you don't)
- They are in a better place
- At least they aren't suffering any longer
- She's with the angels now
- Never make religious or cultural statements in an attempt to comfort them.

Simply be empathic and show support for their situation. Treat them as you would want an investigator treating your spouse, child, or parents.

5. Medical Personnel

It seems that too often, many medical personnel want to hang everything on HIPPA, even when HIPPA does not apply. In many cases health care providers, from a fear of being sued or just a general lack of wanting to help, decline saying anything and blame it on HIPPA. Let me define and explain the HIPPA law.

HIPAA: Acronym that stands for the Health Insurance Portability and Accountability Act, a US law designed to provide privacy standards to protect patient's medical records and other health information provided to health plans, doctors, hospitals and other health care providers. Developed by the Department of Health and Human Services, these standards provide patients with access to their medical records and more control over how their personal health information is used and disclosed. They represent a uniform, federal floor of privacy protections for consumers across the country.

The HIPAA Privacy Rule protects the individually identifiable health information about a decedent for 50 years following the date of death of the individual. During the 50-year period of protection, the Privacy Rule generally protects a decedent's health information to the same extent the Rule protects the health information of living individuals but does include a number of special disclosure provisions relevant to deceased individuals. These include provisions that permit a covered entity to disclose a decedent's health information:

(1) to alert law enforcement to the death of the individual when there is a suspicion that death resulted from criminal conduct (§ 164.512; (2) to coroners, medical examiners and funeral directors (§164.512; (3) for research that is solely on the protected health information of decedents (§ 164.512; and (4) to organ procurement organizations or other entities engaged in the procurement, banking, or transplantation of cadaveric organs, eyes, or tissue for the purpose of facilitating organ, eye, or tissue donation and transplantation (§ 164.512.

You can get certain information from health care providers and medical records personnel. One key factor to keep in mind is, as a law enforcement officer, you may be required to get a subpoena for records pertaining to both the incident in question and any past records. However, keep in mind federal law and most (if not all) states exclude coroners and medical examiners from needing a subpoena if requesting records for the purpose of establishing cause and manner of death. Whereas cause may be obvious, blunt force trauma to the head for example, manner may need more investigation such as past injuries, history of abuse, or medical conditions and disease.

Manner of death includes

- Natural
- Accident
- Homicide
- Suicide
- Undermined

Since the coroner and medical examiner have the same interest you have, which is discovering the truth, they can share information with you as to their determination and how they arrived at that determination.

Building Relationships

With all that said, it is still very important that investigators build solid relationships with Emergency Room staff at local hospitals. Remember that injuries which could be suspected as criminal activity are reportable, whether the patient is dead or alive. Hospitals are mandated reporters in cases of child, domestic, and sexual abuse.

Building relationships with staff will help when you come in with questions. Looking at this from a human condition point of view, we are all more willing to share what we may know with other professionals we deem as our friends. Not so far as breaking any laws, but relationships may prevent the dreaded HIPPA hang-up.

Medical Release Form

You can also obtain records if you have a quality medical release form signed by the victim or the legal guardian of a victim. In most cases these can be served directly to the custodian of records at the medical facility and you will receive your records. Be sure to get this signed as soon as you can, even while at the scene or at first contact whenever possible. These are generally revocable only in writing and when your victim changes their mind in the morning you can still pursue the case. Always act in accordance with your agency guidelines and have a predetermined policy in place with command staff and prosecutors.

6. Area Canvassing

I will admit that conducting an area canvass can be tedious and very time consuming. Sometimes hundreds of contacts are often made without one shred of usable information being unveiled. However, it is that one exhilarating jewel that is occasionally discovered that makes the process so rewarding.

Most criminal investigation courses and books talk little about an area canvass, other than to suggest doing one. There are right and wrong ways to conduct an area canvass that will yield better results for the efforts put out.

Ideally, patrol personnel and plain clothes detectives should perform separate canvasses. Some individuals respond more readily to an authority figure in a uniform, while others prefer the anonymity of the detective's plain clothes. Since it is impossible to know who will respond more willingly to either approach, both should be employed. This technique will give the investigator the greatest chance of getting vital information.

First, understand the terms "area canvass" and "neighborhood canvass" may be used interchangeably. They are interviews conducted in the field, as opposed to statements taken on scene or in the station. The canvass may be conducted in an area near the crime scene or, conceivably, hundreds of miles away from it. In the aftermath of a bank robbery, for example, the getaway vehicle may be located several counties, or even states, away. Two canvasses should therefore be undertaken: one at the original crime scene (the bank) and one at the secondary scene (the vehicle). If a suspect is developed, it may be advisable to perform an additional area canvass in the neighborhood where that person resides to learn about his/her reputation and habits. A complex case may require that a number of area canvasses be completed at various locations.

The main goal of a neighborhood canvass is, of course, to locate a witness to the crime. It is this promise of the elusive witness that motivates the investigator. However, it is not only the "eye" witness you seek. On occasion, it may be just as significant to discover an "ear witness". Someone who may have heard a threatening remark, heard gunshots, or even heard how and in which direction the perpetrator fled.

This information can point the case in the right direction. A witness who hears a homicide subject flee in a vehicle with a loud muffler, for example, could be furnishing a valuable lead. Likewise, intimidating or threatening statements the witness may have overheard could refute a subsequent claim of self-defense. In an officer-involved shooting incident, a witness who hears the officer yell "stop police" or "drop the gun" is invaluable to the investigation. Just as important as the eye-witness or the ear-witness is the "witness-who-knows-a-witness." Even though this person may not have first-hand knowledge of the crime he or she can direct investigators to a person who does and is, therefore, of great value.

Hear say

Rumors, innuendo, and gossip may not have a place in the courtroom, but they are certainly welcome tidbits that help navigate any investigation. The type of approach the investigator uses to cultivate this information can often determine how successful he will be. In certain situations, it may be necessary to coax and cajole the witness. In others, it may be beneficial to appear to confide in the witness and reveal some "inside scoop" about the investigation. This works particularly well with the neighborhood "busy body" who will derive motivation from being "included" in the case. Also, remember that in certain situations an area canvass may more resemble an interrogation than a simple interview. Eliciting information from a witness, who is not predisposed to furnish it, is the essence of any area canvass.

In high crime, drug infested neighborhoods retaliation for "snitching" to the police is a real life possibility that must be appreciated. Witnesses who refuse or are reluctant to cooperate with authorities may have ample reason for their trepidation. That is why each person approached should be provided with a contact number and assurances that they may remain anonymous.

Empathy and friendliness

When initial contact is made with the witness, the investigators should politely introduce themselves and explain why they are there. They should try to convey to the witness how potentially important their information might be even though, to them, it may seem like no big deal. Every effort should be made to personalize the event by offering such observations as, "they could have just as easily broken into your house" or "imagine if your kids were outside when all that shooting took place" or "they could have robbed *your* mother."

If the witness invites the investigator into his/her residence, this invitation should ***always*** be accepted. This is vitally important. In fact, every effort should be made ***to*** be invited in. The reason for this is twofold. First, the witness may feel more comfortable talking away from the prying eyes of others in the neighborhood. Secondly, it is human nature for a person to be more polite, more accommodating and more gracious to a guest in his/her home.

Similarly, if the witness asks the investigator to sit down, he/she should do so. If the standard reply to this request is, "no thank you sir, I really don't have time," this implies to the potential witness that the inquiry being made must not really be that important. It also conveys an indirect disrespect to the homeowner. Make the person being questioned feel as though they have the undivided attention of the questioner. If the witness offers refreshments, (coffee, tea, water), they too, should always be accepted. Accepting the witness's hospitality reinforces the notion that, as a guest in their home, the questioner should be treated cordially and respectfully.

It has been repeatedly proven that a skilled interviewer must also be an adept listener. Never cut off a witness who appears to be rambling. That person may just be nervous and simply meandering until they are able to control their apprehensions. Moreover, seemingly any stories regarding suspicious vehicles or persons in the neighborhood, that occurred days or weeks earlier, may actually be worthwhile leads when scrutinized. The bottom line…never discount ***any*** information received during a canvass.

7. Interviewing Children

Interviewing children, whereas some similarities exist, much of how you will conduct these interviews are very different and will require additional legal aspects and approach. You may be in a situation where you will be talking to a juvenile – whatever age that is for your state or jurisdiction. Most jurisdictions define a juvenile as an individual under the age of 18. Some states however, such as in Missouri, define a juvenile as anyone not yet reaching their 17th birthday. Then of course you have the issues of mental capabilities, the age when crime was committed, versus the age when the subject was questioned, and other such restrictions. You need to be sure you are familiar with your state's laws regarding interviewing and especially interrogating juveniles.

Children can fall into three basic categories of persons:

1. Witness
2. Victim
3. Suspect

Each one will be defined by differing laws and restrictions. In this book I will be dealing with general guidelines and practices. Always consult with your prosecuting attorney to know in advance what rules apply and when they apply.

Sometimes you have to talk with children on scene or in an emergency situation. Never shy away from talking to kids, they are full of information and many are willing to share. Your approach must be calm and protective to smaller children and you must show concern and understanding with older children. Teens require you meeting them on their level. Keep in mind that this age child has already made a lot of conclusions about their world, their situation, and how they feel about your profession. You will need to earn their trust and respect.

Children as Witnesses

Parents are generally not required to be present when you are talking with children as witnesses. This is especially true in cases of expedience, such as seeing a group of kids playing near a crime scene. These kids may have very important time sensitive information. Be sure to gather all parent contact details so you can re-contact them later if needed.

If talking to children at school, you may find the need to advise parents ahead of time. However, in many cases, this is not necessary. For example, if you are gathering important information the child may have and waiting is not a clear option. School officials may be reluctant and finesse may be needed.

A word of caution about parents; whenever possible, and certainly as soon as possible afterwards, contact the parents to let them know that you have spoken to their child and why. NEVER remove a child (witness) from their present location without informing parents. This includes kids on the street as well as in school, unless of course their safety is in question. Then notify parents as soon as possible as to the location of their child and what steps the parents need to take next.

Children as Suspects

When you are talking with a child suspected of committing a crime, you are conducting an interrogation. In these cases, laws such as juvenile Miranda warnings, including the state juvenile officer, and having parents present with the child come into play.

You will need to work to gain the trust of parents. Most parents are protective of their children even when they know their child has done wrong. Parents may understand the need for consequences, but will still look out for the best interest of their child – as it should be!

Interrogation techniques can be employed in the same manner as we will discuss in the interrogation section of this book. Your only difference will be the afore mentioned additional aspects.

Children as Victims

Why should you ever talk to children as victims? Often times you may be first on the scene and need to gain some initial information. Do not delay in speaking to a child. Keep in mind that many children are afraid of cops and believe what parents and others have said negatively about law enforcement. You will need to work to gain their trust. Remember why you are there in the first place, these kids are scared and confused, help them relax.

Building trust and rapport

Approach children on their level, literally. Get on the floor or ground with them. Never stand over them in an authoritative manner. This is age dependent of course, but the importance here is to be seen as less threatening or frightening. There have been many times where I have actually sat cross-legged on the ground next to a child to have a conversation. Spend some time making small talk. Talk about things that interest them like their dog, sports, games, or the toy they are playing with. Become a real person in their eyes not a cop.

Getting information

Specific interview techniques and skills may require you to have some advanced training specializing in child interviews. If you are working a case of child abuse and have the opportunity to take the child to a Family Advocacy Center or similar agency skilled in having forensic conversations with children, then do so. However, what I am talking about here are those times when a child wants to talk now, why shut them up? Or in cases where immediate initial information is be needed.

Avoid using truth / lie statement questions. This can confuse the child and can cause them to believe you already don't trust them. Just see what they know, what their story is or what their version of events is 'in their words'. Let them talk, you can always verify statements after your conversation. Take good notes, an audio recording may be helpful here, not only in helping your memory, but also in allowing others to review the conversation and prevent re-interviews.

A word of caution; children are easily influenced. If a child makes a statement to you such as "my daddy touched me down there" and you respond with "are you sure?"; you have now placed the child in a defensive position and they can feel like you do not approve and may change their story. I'm not saying we believe everything on face value that comes from a child's mouth, which is why you investigate the case. However, the child needs to feel they are being believed. Their trust has already been damaged in some way, and you are trying to get them to trust you, essentially calling them a liar in the first conversation may greatly damage your case in the future.

Watch out for the "Then What" conversations

With younger children you need to be careful how you construct your conversation. In an attempt to gain full details in a chronological order we often times make the mistake of asking 'then what' questions after each statement the child makes. Doing this can cause the child to embellish the story because they feel you want more or they are enjoying the conversation. For example, with my 3-year-old granddaughter, she can be telling me something and if I act interested and ask "then what", she will be glad to tell me. The more I ask "then what", the more she tells. It's not long before the story is taking some real imaginative paths. But she is enjoying my interest and wants to continue the conversation. Instead, form your non-leading questions in such a way that the child will have to answer with better than yes / no answers. If you need more detailed information, ask the question you want to know. For example

"my daddy touched me down there"
"where is down there, can you point to where that is"
"how did daddy touch you"
"with his hand"
"did daddy say anything to you while he was touching you"
"he said it was okay because I was a big girl now and he was teaching me things"
"what did daddy do while touching you"
"he put his finger inside me"
"where did daddy put his finger inside"
"you know , down there in my 'gina where I pee"
"what did daddy do after he put his finger inside your 'gina" (always use their words)
"I told him he was hurting me and he took it out"
"what did daddy do then, after he took his finger out"
"nothing, he just left the room"

Continue with this type of conversation. Again, in each case every child will be different. Specialized skills are a must. But the main point I want to make about talking with children is to have a conversation with them, make them feel safe, and get your information.

Older children, or children with higher intellectual development can often times simply tell you the story from start to finish. Do not interrupt them. Go back and ask clarifying questions when they are done if needed, but let them tell the story in their words completely the first time.

Why talk to child victims at all?

I often get asked why we should even talk to kids, let the experts at CAC or some other agency do it. I agree! However, there are times when you must get initial information from a child and waiting can cause the child to change their story or be influenced by other adults. If a child is willing to talk, there is no harm in listening, even if you don't conduct a full forensic interview. You need to make assessments regarding their safety and gain vital scene information. What if they are still living with the perpetrator and you shut them up and send them back home to daddy, just to have them re-abused? This includes, but is certainly not limited to, sexual assault. Children are victims of many types of crime, not just sexual crime. For instance, what if a child was in a car subsequent to a car-jacking and was later found dropped off a few miles away. Would you not want to talk with this 'kidnapped' victim as soon as possible?

Part Two

Suspect Interrogation

8. Interrogations Custody and Miranda

Before we can start any discussion on interrogations and techniques we must first define the legal parameters of an interrogation. An interrogation, as opposed to an interview, takes place when you are asking guilt seeking questions. During an interrogation, the subject to which you are speaking is in custody and you have a belief that they have committed a crime. When both of these exist, guilty seeking questions and custody, Miranda warning is required prior to asking any guilt seeking questions.

Let's define custody. Custody is not always how you, the investigator, sees it. The question you must answer in court would be – could a group of reasonable people believe the subject was in custody or not? This is regardless of your opinion or attitude toward the situation; the question of custody is determined by the circumstances, reasonable appearance of the environment, and what the subject could reasonably believe.

Even if you have told the subject they are not under arrest and were free to leave, they might still assume they are in custody depending on their location and surroundings. For instance, sitting in the back of a police car could be assumed custody. Standing on the street with two or three officers could also be assumed custody. People are told not to run from police, they are told they must answer questions when asked. It's the brave rare person that would just push through a group of officers and walk off. If you place a hand out to stop them – you have just made a detention and thus custody can be assumed. If you call a suspect on the phone or they call you, custody in most cases can never be assumed. Remember, the answer of custody is in how the suspect sees it, not you, and will be judged by how a group of ordinary people might interpret it.

If you have the slightest question of whether the Miranda warning should be given, then give it. I will show you later how to do this in a legal manner but in a way not to cause alarm to the suspect. Giving a Miranda warning correctly will not automatically stop a conversation. However, it is better to stop the conversation than to get a confession that will be suppressed in court.

Guilt seeking questions: The law allows you to have a conversation with a suspect about anything until the point of 'guilt seeking questions'. For example, basic information such as name, contact information, employment, family, kids, sports, and even small talk can be discussed outside of Miranda. You can even talk about the case and present facts of the case, as long as you are not asking questions which could lead to his guilt. No Miranda is necessary for them to sit and listen.

I have heard of cases where suspects have been asked to come to a police station and talk with an investigator. The investigator advised the subject they were not under arrest and could simply walk out anytime they wanted. The investigator had even had the subject sign a form stating his acknowledgment of this. In many jurisdictions this has held up in court. It is a risky venture but if waded into under the approval of a prosecuting attorney you're probably on solid ground.

However, consider for a moment my agency. The subject comes to the front lobby and tells the person behind the glass they are there to see me. They get 'buzzed' in through a locked door to the main lobby where they wait for me. I come down and escort the person upstairs via the elevator. Upon arriving at the second floor I use my key fob to unlock a second door. We walk down the hall to the investigation division area where I again use my fob to open the third locked door and enter the investigations area. When we arrive at the interview rooms I smoothly use my fob to open the interview room door and invite them in. I tell them to have a seat and I will be right back. I go and get my file, return and advise them they are not under arrest and are free to leave at any time. Would a reasonable person believe that? How many locked doors did they just get escorted through? Now, they do not know it, but each door will open just fine from the inside and he could be out in the parking lot in no time and with no help from me, but how could he be expected to know that?

Now let's consider this option, you ask to meet someone at the local diner for a conversation; you have arrived before them and have driven in an unmarked vehicle, you are dressed in plain clothes, no uniform. When they arrive they join you at the table and you advise them they are not under arrest and are free to leave anytime, you just want to have a conversation. During the course of your conversation he makes admissions or even a confession about the crime. Could custody be assumed to a group of ordinary people, probably not. However, this again is a slippery slope. We have all done this and it has worked, but it just as easily can backfire.

Advising Miranda: When possible, as in a controlled interview room, advise Miranda warning from a preprinted form and have them sign the form acknowledging their understanding. In other situations, always advise Miranda warning from a preprinted card that you always carry with you (even to court). Never, never, never give Miranda from memory. You will be embarrassed in court someday if you do, trust me! Also be sure to note and document time Miranda was given, if given more than once, document time of each occurrence.

9. Preparing for Interrogation

Before you can conduct any successful interrogation there are some steps you must take to prepare. This preparation begins with the very first contact ANY officer has with the suspect. The methods of interrogations laid out in this book are geared toward gaining trust, confidence, and building rapport. This will fall apart rather quickly if the patrol officers you send out to pick the guy up treat him like garbage.

All patrol officers and investigators must be trained in how to talk to and prepare suspects. If a suspect is arrested, then talked down to or mistreated in any way or even disrespected, how willing do you think he will be to talk to you later? He is already mad and will likely lawyer up pretty fast. Transporting officers must have careful, or no conversation during transport back to the office.

The next two big steps in preparing for an interrogation are facts of the case and background of the suspect. Let's take an in-depth look at each of these.

Facts of the case

As the one doing an interrogation you must know every fact possible about a case. Obviously the bigger and more high profile the case the better you should know it. However, every case requires the investigator to know as much as they can before talking to a suspect. How will you know when the lie comes if he knows more about the case than you do?

Review all reports and supplemental writings

Prior to talking with suspects, you need to know as much as you can about what the reporting officer knew and what results laboratory and CSI work found. If possible, talk directly to the reporting officer and get a sense of what they saw and knew at the scene.

Read all witness statements

The interrogator will want to know everything any witnesses has said about the incident and how they saw it. If someone can place the suspect at the scene or adds to or detracts from an alibi, you need to know that before you start your conversation with a suspect. The suspect will not know what knowledge you have of the case. This will give you an advantage during the interrogation.

Crime scene photos, sketches, and videos

If you can go to an actual scene, regardless of how long it has been since the crime, try to do this prior to meeting with the suspect. You can then review photos even while on the scene to give you a much better perspective of what the photos are trying to convey. Let me give you an example; which is better- me giving you some photos of my beach front vacation to look at, or you looking at those photos while actually on the beach. Which one do you think will give you a better understanding of what I saw, smelled, and felt? Same with crime scenes, you need to know what the scene was like. If the crime happened in the dark, be sure to go back in the day time as well as after dark so that you can get a real sense of the scene.

If going to the scene is just not possible, then be sure you become very familiar with the photos and videos. You need to know as much as you can about how things looked and where things took place. This includes the relative size of rooms, where the crime was committed, the window the suspect came in, etc. If you see a window too small for the 400 pound man you're getting ready to talk to, you may have a different set of questions.

Background of suspect

You need to know the suspect better than they know themselves. Prior to entering the room with the suspect, you need to know their arrest history, jail conduct reports, medical issues, drug and alcohol offenses and addictions, family status (married, divorced, parents alive or dead, was father in the home, childhood abuse, any siblings and their current status, etc.), religious affiliations or lack of any, employment history or lack of, and military time if any.

The interrogator simply has to know everything they can about the suspect and the facts surrounding the crime and the scene. Knowing this information not only gives you the power of knowledge, it will be very helpful during the interrogation to present suggestive evidence or make reason formulation with the suspect.

10. Developing a Plan

One thing is for sure, you must have a plan BEFORE you enter the room if you want to get confessions, you cannot wing it in there. Over my 30 years of working criminal investigation I have come to learn this principal; not that some confession might be obtained by some form of "winging it". By and large the investigators that get the most confessions, and the least amount of problems later in court, are the ones who have a solid plan before ever stepping in front of a suspect in an interrogation room.

The least you want

Decide what the least amount of admission or confession you want before you begin. If you hit a road block and do not get a full confession, what can you get him to admit? Maybe he agrees he was there but he didn't steal anything. He had sex with her but she consented. He sat in the car, but the other guy was in the house when the victim was shot.

Most suspects never give every little detail anyway, and in most states the criminal code will charge and convict even if the suspect admits being present, not under duress, and fails to report the crime. I've sent several duos to jail and each one blamed the other for the actual final act.

Reason formulation

We will talk at length about reason formulation in chapter 13. But for now, let me say that while in the plan development stage you can use the facts that you know from the case to pre-decide some "either/or" statements. Reason formulation plan can also be used when the opportunity presents itself. These will be based upon your knowledge of the suspect and the facts of the case.

Using props

Props are always the best part of the planning process. If you decide to use props, be sure to have them prepared and ready for when you walk in the room. Carry them into the room in a box or file folder. Know what you are using them for and when they should be played. Be sure to never let the suspect 'see your hand', just let him notice that you have stuff. You can present or refer to this 'evidence' later in the interrogation. Props, in essence, are suggestive evidence that fit the case and the suspect's actions and activities while committing the crime or soon afterward.

I better explain what props are; props, as in a play, are items that appear real but in fact are simply make believe to fit the scenario you are presenting. Could the suspect be on video surveillance that he did not know about? Have a DVD, marked appropriately, "accidently" slide from a file folder onto the table. Pick it up just after the suspect was able to read what was written on the disc. Say nothing more about it unless it comes up later or fits.

Several copies of signed witness statements in a file look great when talking about witnesses, never mind how many old cases you used to copy those statements from. Have any old fingerprint evidence lying around, or have some you made? These work great to appear as evidence.

Props can be used over and over depending on the facts of the case. Make yourself a props kit and store it in your office. When your putting an interrogation plan together pull from your stash to help develop your plan.

Use caution, however, when presenting these props. If you are not completely familiar with the case and the suspect, a prop can backfire. You may get to a point where you have nothing to lose but to play your card. But in most cases play it smart and use it when it fits, how it fits, and know that it cannot be factually disputed by the suspect.

Using Audio / Video

Any audio or video you are using needs to be set up prior to the suspect being placed in the interrogation room. No need to make him more nervous by knowing that you are setting up recording equipment. He needs to feel this conversation is between you and him. People share secrets better in private. If your interrogation room is not designed with pre-installed equipment, then set up what you are using as covertly as you can. A video camera in his face from the first moment will hinder his openness.

Documenting the interrogation

Every interrogation needs to have certain things carefully documented. These need to be recorded as they occur and then written in your final report after you have gotten the confession.

- Start time
- Time Miranda was given – even if given more than once
- Breaks - restroom, food, drink
- Who came into room – when and why?
- What time did the first admission come?
- What time did the confession come, or start?
- What time did the interrogation end?
- What happened after the interrogation – arrested, sent home, taken back to jail, etc.

Polygraph or CVSA (computerized voice stress analysis)

Decide in advance if you plan to offer this to a suspect. If you are an examiner you can offer and conduct right way. But never offer this early in the interrogation unless you can give it. If he says he will take one and you have to wait several days to schedule it, you may have lost your chance to get him to confess. Remember, he does not leave that room until he confesses, legally of course, but do not give reasons early on for him to stop talking to you.

Setting up the room

An interrogation room should be set up in a certain way for a specific purpose. Some agencies do not have the luxury of having a dedicated room for interrogations. For many years, when I first became a detective, I had to use my own office to do interrogations. This worked but I had to modify some things each time. Still, it was not ideal due to not being able to leave the suspect alone, and having to always be concerned with what else was on my desk or shelves. I had to be concerned about what could be used as a weapon or what other case file might be in view. You can do it, but you have to use some extra caution.

Regardless of the room you use, some things are important in every situation. Always have minimal chairs. It is best to be one-on-one when possible. Secrets are best told to only one person. But if another investigator needs to be in the room (s)he must sit, NO ONE STANDS. Place the other investigator behind the suspect and out of sight. Have a small desk or table sitting next to you. Never interrogate across a desk or table. Position the table so that each of you are near an end.

This will come into play when you have to move close or use touching techniques at key times. Plus, sitting across a desk gives too much authority figure status to the investigator.

Also important, the suspect sits on a hard chair with straight legs. You on the other hand should have rollers on your chair because you will need mobility when you have to get close to him to talk.

If interviewing an opposite sex suspect, you might want another person in the room, although it is best if they can monitor from CCTV or glass when possible. A male police officer and a female suspect can be a recipe for unwanted allegations.

Another thing to keep in mind about the room you use, regardless of what type, is that it must be quite and free from distractions. Be sure you have a policy in place that NO ONE disturbs you unless the building is on fire, everything else can wait.

Room design

The room used for interrogations needs to be scantly furnished; it's not made to be comfortable. No windows in the room or if there are ensure they are covered to prevent sound and sight distractions. The walls should be painted a neutral color; light grey, tan, or pale blue. But never; red, green, black, or any bold colors. Study about the affects of color on human psychology and you will see why this is important. Also you should have one color for all walls, no need for colorful accent walls in here.

The room should be well lit and the light evenly distributed throughout the room. The old movies with a single bulb hanging from the ceiling over the suspect is stuff for Hollywood not real police work.

11. Your First Contact

Your first contact with a suspect may be the most important one. Take a moment before you enter the room and prepare your attitude. Keep in mind this is a cat and mouse game and salesmanship is going to be key for you getting your confession. Be sure you can mentally do this. If this happens to be a child sexual assault case ask yourself if you can really handle this. Some officers simply cannot show the empathy and feign the proper attitude to talk with certain suspects. You must walk into that room confident yet relaxed and ready to be their friend. If you can't do this, do not go into that room.

Your first priority is to get the suspect comfortable. Ask if they would like anything to drink or eat – if so be sure someone gets it right away. Do not delay in having someone fill this request, is not a reward this is building rapport. You may want to do this a few minutes before you enter the room for the interrogation. If it has been a while since he has eaten, let him get that out of the way first. His concentration needs to be on you and not a cheese burger.

Take him to the restroom prior to starting if needed, be sure to document this. After drinking his soda you just got for him he will need to go later as well, you can use that to your advantage then. However, you will want him comfortable and relaxed starting out.

Initial conversation

When you first enter the room introduce yourself. Your title may or may not be important, you can decide that. Some officers simply use their first name and introduce themselves as an investigator. Start with small talk; name, address, educational background, personal history, kids, employment, family, etc. This small talk does two things: first it helps to break the ice on conversation, and you are both sizing each other up while he is forming an opinion of you. Secondly, it gets the conversation happening, and you are also able to get a sense of his attitude and cooperation, while gauging his honesty on things you should already know. If you find an attitude issue or a reluctance to talk, its better to start overcoming this now in relatively unimportant matters before getting to the real issues.

Keep in mind this initial small talk is not just fact gathering. You do not simply want to know if he has kids and what their names are. This is not a "just the facts ma'am" conversation. If he has kids talk about them; what are their names, do they like sports, if so what kind, does he help coach, how are they in school? Is he married; how long, how did they meet? He's divorced; oh I'm sorry to hear that, it's got to be tough. If he expands then you expand. You are trying to get to know the suspect. How well does he communicate, are all his answers short or does he like to expand – you will gauge these answers against the ones that really matter later. If he is real chatty about kids and work, yet goes to one word answers later, you might be getting close to the hot issue. The reverse is also true; if he just grunts answers about his kids and job, or seems disinterested in friendly conversation, yet later on won't shut up about his alibi, facts as he knows them, and every reason under the sun why he is not your man, you will notice the change and know that you are on the right track.

Handling Miranda

After spending some time in small talk you will come to a point where you will have to advise the suspect of his Miranda rights. Tell the suspect that it is very important you hear his side of the story. You only have one side and there are always two sides, and you are very interested in hearing his side so this thing can be cleared up. You need to do this in such a way as to minimize its impact. Always advise from a pre-printed form and simply read the form and ask him if he understands and have him sign the form. You do not need to spend a great deal of time explaining each point, just read the form ask him if he understand and wishes to proceed and move on.

Your attitude is important here. Tell him something like, "Hey, you know, just like on TV I have to read your rights. It's no big deal, but to be fair to you let me read them." After you have read them and he has signed the form, PUT IT AWAY. Place the form in a drawer, a file folder or under the desk. I don't care where but he does not need to see that form again until court.

Advising the Miranda warning is important and is his constitutional right. You have to do it to have your confession hold up in court. But no where is there a rule that this has to be some big production. Minimize its effects and stay light hearted about it. You are friends now, so just get it out of the way and move on.

Your opening statements

After Miranda is out of the way, it's time to put the ball into play. Your next words are critical. You can open up the conversation or close it down before you ever get started. Never use words that will scare the suspect, I have heard them referred to as "frightening words". Words such as murder, rape, burglary, child molestation, these words mean prison time. They produce fear and will put the legal system back into their minds. You have spent a lot of time getting him to relax and trust you, don't ruin it by reminding him he's going to prison. You need to consider how the suspect is feeling. How would you feel?

Open with a statement like, I need to talk to you about:

The house you went into (Burglary)
That girl you had sex with (Rape)
The guy you took money from (Robbery – Theft)
That car you borrowed (Car Theft)
This problem you are having with urges (Child sexual abuse)

Also minimize the crime "IT'S NO BIG DEAL IT HAPPENS ALL THE TIME". That phrase needs to become your guiding phrase in every interrogation every time.

12. Interrogation Technique

Do this right and you will get a confession 90% of the time

Remember, you do not have to have every last detail, nor will you get it every single time. Often if you can place them at the scene by their admission, they're convicted.

- I only drove.
- I had sex with her but she said she was 18.
- John shot the guy. I didn't know he was going to.
- We only went in to look around I didn't know John was going to take anything.
- He hit me first and I only hit back.

All of these admissions put him at the scene and will usually be enough to convict. I'm not saying you don't push forward, but get what you can. If it helps him minimize this issue for the time being, let him admit to what he can.

Never argue

Never, never, never, argue with a suspect. If he says he didn't do it, never start the - yes you did, no I didn't stand off. Remember they are supposed to lie to you, its their part of the game, your part of the game is to help them over it.

At this point in the interrogation process you have three goals. These goals will proceed in order but you may have to double back and start over several times to get to the confession.

You must get the suspect to :

1. Talk
2. Admit
3. Confess

If at some point during the interrogation the admissions are not coming or the suspect is starting to show aggression, you may want to circle back to the top and just talk again. Talk about whatever you found he was interested in at an earlier point. Maybe it was family, maybe kids, or maybe it is the crime itself, but you want to circle him back around to his denial and go over the details again. If they are saying they were not involved, then ask why or how it is they were not involved. Your goal is to keep the suspect talking, if he is not talking he will never admit or confess.

Running out the alibi

Suspects will often have alibis as to why they could not have committed a crime or have been where you are saying they were at the time you are saying. If a suspect has such a story, then you will need to run it out completely. You will need to get the entire alibi in this interrogation and run it out <u>before</u> he leaves. Running out the alibi does not mean he says he was at his girlfriends house and you say okay, you need details.

If he was at his girlfriend's house, you need her name and address, time he arrived and left, what did they do from the time he arrived to the time he left? Did they watch a movie? Which one, did they rent it, where, was it on Netflix or Red Box DVD? Did they eat in or order out? Had pizza delivered, what kind of pizza, from where, what time did it arrive, who paid, how paid, what did it cost? Did you use your cell phone during the time you were at your girlfriend's house? Who called or text, who did you call or text? Did anyone arrive at the house while you were there, was anyone else at the house already, what was the weather like, on, and on, and on.

Verifying the alibi

The alibi must be verified right away. Do not let the suspect leave and think you will call him back after you check on some details of his story. It's late, you're tired, and you just want to go home. You'll just start verifying tomorrow, right? This is where those who get confessions and those who don't, differ. You need to get everything in one sitting. You send him home or back to his cell and the chances of you getting a confession later has dropped to less than 30%.

At this point give him a break. He stays right where he is; but get him something to eat or drink, let him use the restroom and smoke if he needs to. He can then cool his heels in the interrogation room while you and another investigator start verifying. Call his girlfriend, or send a patrol officer to her house in order to get details of that time frame. Call the pizza joint and have them check orders for that night. If this is a big enough case, get the manager out of bed and get him back to the store. Was the delivery made and does it match the details the suspect gave you? Look into the suspect's cell phone, you may need a search warrant for this, or his permission. If it's normal office hours, start the process of getting records from the phone company. Check television listings to see if what he said he watched was on. If there was a Red Box rental, who rented it? Verify the purchase. If in a public place, check to see if there is any video of area. If he told you someone else was there or arrived, talk to that person, you may have to verify their location as well.

My point is this, you must check every detail of his story. Never take a suspect's word for an alibi, its your job to <u>verify everything.</u>

Destroying the alibi

Now that you have his full details and you have verified everything you can over the past couple hours, return to the interrogation room and start the ball game again. If during your verification you found holes, inconsistencies, or outright lies, you are in prime position to get the confession. Since he has given you every detail of that time frame and you have run it completely and have found many things to be false, he has nowhere to turn. It's not like he just said he was at his girlfriend's house and lied. He could just say he got the day wrong and instead he was at work, now you're back to square one. However, since he gave you every detail of that time frame then he is backed into a corner.

Find holes in his story and work on those holes, prove them wrong and prove to him you know he is lying. If you know he is lying and can prove it through other means, then present that to him. Also here's a trick, if you're convinced and have the facts that you know he is your guy, make something up. Yes, lie to him, he's been lying to you for five hours its fair game you have a turn. Tell him you checked with the dispatch center and there was a large fight at a party next to his girlfriend's house that night and everyone in the area was talked to by patrol officers. Why had he not mentioned that, or why had his name not been on the list, they show that they talked to everyone at your girlfriend's house. Be careful with these kind of stories, they could backfire, but if you know good and well he was not there then he does not know if what you're saying happened or not. Things like this can get him to a place of resolve. If you destroy the alibi, you then start over with the talking phase and move forward.

Empathy and Concern

At this point in the interrogation process you have built some rapport and may have destroyed an alibi if he had one. Throughout the entire interrogation you must show empathy and concern for him and his situation. Be his friend in that room, never let him know how you really feel about him or his crime. Tell him you understand and ITS NO BIG DEAL, IT HAPPENS ALL THE TIME.

Use examples of other cops, your brother, sister-in-law, son, or even yourself as someone who has made a similar mistake. People make mistakes all the time, ITS NO BIG DEAL!

Remember, depending on the level of crime, he really wants to get this off his chest. He wants to tell someone, he needs resolve. What he does not want, and what he is afraid of, is going to jail. Help him minimize that fear. Don't promise him he won't serve jail time, but minimize that part of it.

I'll tell you a story that worked a lot and is completely legal. I have told suspects that if they fully cooperated with me and told me every detail so that we could clear this matter up, I would be sure to tell the prosecuting attorney that he cooperated fully and was sincerely sorry for what happened. I would remind him that it is illegal for me to make promises I could not keep. I would also be sure to emphasis that he told me that he 'thought she was 18', 'that he only was there but didn't shoot the guy', whatever; and that I would be sure that every bit of that was in my report. I would even go so far as to allow him to write in his statement that I had promised him I would do these things for him. I would be sure that I did put in my report that he was cooperative and that he did say he was sorry and that he had stated such and such.

The law forbids you from making promises to suspects during an interrogation that you cannot keep or have no authority to ensure. For instance, I could not legally promise him only probation, or lighter a sentence. Those things are completely out of my hands. However, it is perfectly legal to make promises I can keep and can control as long as I can prove I did indeed fulfill those promises. Those promises were fulfilled in my report and I even allowed him to put it at the end of his statement. Perfectly legal, and this also gives the suspect some comfort in hoping it helps his case. Further, I have continued to show empathy and concern for him and built further rapport.

13. Reason Formulation and Either / Or statements

Reason formulation is probably the most important aspect of an interrogation; second only to your attitude. Suspects want to blame someone or something for why they committed a crime. This helps them reason with what they did and makes them feel better about it in hopes others will feel sorry them. It also gives them a way to show they are not really such a bad guy, if it had not been for such and such then I would have never done the crime, I'm not that sort of guy.

In reason formulation we blame everyone and everything for why they did what they did. Phrases like:

- Bob pulled you into it.
- You would have never….. but he hit you first and then just kept taunting you.
- Job loss – you have a family to support.
- She led you on – making out until the critical moment, how could anyone just stop?
- Drugs or alcohol – controls you, you wish you could stop.
- You have these urges you do not like but cannot control.

Back these reasons up with reason statements:

- I understand, it happens all the time, it's no big deal
- You're a good guy and would never….. without cause
- In a moment of weakness.
- My brother-in-law, neighbor kid, son, or other cop, etc. did the same thing.
- We had a case just last week – give details of this "similar case".
- You were drunk/high, it's not your fault, you would never have otherwise.
- Blame drugs – you're hooked and have to have money, it's not your fault.
- Someone with your problem needs counseling not jail.

Either / Or Statement

Along with reason formulation, offer the suspect a way out of his behavior with an either/or statement. These work extremely well and are just another way of allowing him to minimize his actions in hopes others will as well. These statements will go to his admission; they are not a way out of guilt. Either choice he makes, he's guilty.

Give him options like:

- Either you're the leader or a follower.
- Either you planned this whole thing or John did.
- Either this was an accident or intentional.
- Either this was a spur of the moment deal or you planned it.
- Either you just lost control of yourself or you meant to do it.
- Either this was the first time or you do this all the time.
- Either you were just defending yourself or you started it.

14. Silence, Crying, and Touch

Silence

Silence is a powerful tool in any conversation. Most of us like to talk and we want to spend time telling the suspect all the reasons he should confess and helping him with reason formulation and either/or statements, yet we never shut up long enough to let the suspect tell us what we have been trying to get him to say.

Most human nature is to fill conversation gaps with talk rather than silence. In this situation you need to say what you need him to hear and then be quiet. When he is talking let him talk, if he takes a pause you be still and in a moment he will start talking again. This can seem like a long time but wait him out. Look at your watch and don't do or say anything for 30 seconds.. It's a long time isn't it? If you can wait it out he will say something most of the time and in most cases he will start expanding on what he just told you.

Suspect silence can be caused for a few reasons

- He is buying into your techniques and is trying to figure out how to confess.
- He is trying to figure out how NOT to confess.
- He is just tuning you out.
- He just doesn't want to talk anymore, for whatever reason.

When this happens, make eye contact. You will get a real sense of what he is thinking this way. Watch body position, posture, and facial expressions. If you're still in the game wait him out a little longer.

Crying

Crying is a good sign. If the suspect starts to cry, DO NOT give them a chance to regain their composure. Keep him crying, he is broken and wants to confess. Change your voice to a low pitch and move in close. Once you're close to him, put your hand on his shoulder and tell him you can understand how he must feel. That its just the two of you and you are here to help him. Say something to get him talking. Give him one of your reason statements or either/or choices. Let him agree to one of those and then ask him to just tell you what happened. He will likely give you only a very small sentence like, "I never meant to hurt anyone" or "if I tell you, you will be mad at me", yes I have had suspects tell me that. I guess my friendship building worked.

Touch

Touching is an important human feeling and emotion, especially during stressful times. Appropriate touch shows your compassion and empathy for the suspect and his situation. Remember, you are his friend, and besides – this is no big deal, it happens all the time!

During a critical point in an interrogation, such as in a crying stage or any other stress moment, touch can push him over the edge to confession. Put your hand on his knee and pat his knee. Touch his upper arm or shoulder. Leave your hand on his shoulder and move in a little closer.

When you are interrogating someone of the opposite sex caution should be used. I am not saying you cannot touch. However, when, where, and how become more critical. Touching an upper arm or shoulder is still fine, especially when on video. What you are wanting to avoid are claims of inappropriate sexual touching. Opposite sex interrogators should avoid touching legs and thighs for sure.

15. Taking the Confession

Once you get to the point in your interrogations when its time to actually take the suspect's confession you are faced with some options as to how best to document it. Obviously you have three choices: oral, written, and audio/video. Each situation will be different and may require you to use all three, or may limit you to only one.

Oral

This may be the only documentation you get unless your interrogation room is equipped with audio/ video from the start. But when taking an oral confession, have the suspect tell you his story in his own words. Let him talk and you take notes. Don't interrupt him at this point just let him talk. After he is finished, go back and fill in the gaps and details. He will have usually left out some important facts. If you have prepared like I discussed in earlier chapters, you will know the case as well as or better than he does, you will see the holes pretty fast. Take him back through the story using the cognitive interview approach and ask clarifying questions to fill in the gaps. Do this casually, be empathic and non-threatening.

When writing your final report of the interrogation you will summarize and quote what the suspect told you, using his own words in much of it. You will build the case that he knew details only the suspect could know. Be sure to write your final report with much detail as possible. Keep in mind as you are writing, his attorney will most likely get him to recant and then it's just your word against his. Your report and integrity will be the benchmark as to whether or not it stands in court.

Written

When possible, get the suspect to write his confession after you have heard it from him in oral story form. Don't expect this to be a novel, you might be lucky to get a half page of text. It is best to have the statement written in chronological order. However you may have to ask him to fill in some important details at the end. You will need to read the statement and be sure all details proving his involvement and your facts are noted, regardless of the final order.

Does he write it or do you?

In most cases it is always best to have him write the statement, regardless of how short it is. However, you can write it and have him sign it, but keep in mind that if he can't write he probably can't read, will this be a valid statement? Another option is to have the confession portion of your recorded interview transcribed and then have him sign it. If you're going to do this, it has to be done right now. If you wait a couple days for someone to get it done, he likely won't sign it.

Audio/Video

The best option is to have an oral confession backed up by a written statement, all while being recorded. What can be a problem is setting up a camera or recording device after he has confessed. The time it takes will likely change his attitude and he may refuse. Another drawback is that attorneys love to point out that the only recording is of a "broken suspect" after hours of intense interrogation and the only thing the court sees is a ten-minute confession. His defense team will adlib the prior hours, and not to your credit.

If you do have a need or occasion, as I have had, to record a confession after the fact you must do a couple things. Be sure that you introduce everyone in the room, giving the time and date the recording starts. Refer to the signed Miranda form you last used, showing it to him, and ask him if he remembers signing it and if he is still willing to talk with you. Ask him if any promises or threats have been made to him. If he reminds you that you told him you would let the prosecutor know he cooperated, agree that you did and this video will help show that he did in fact cooperate.

Then tell him something like, "we are here to talk again about those houses you went into." You have given me a statement but I want to be sure I have your story correct, tell me again about that day. Ask questions if needed and refer to your notes. After you are done be sure to again state the time and date completed.

Covert Recordings

If your interrogation room is equipped with audio and/or video keep in mind that the entire recording is part of the case. You cannot simply splice out the part where he confesses; you will likely get your confession kicked out of court. Also if you have had some time breaks in recording you need to have good explanation for that. This will leave room for defense attorneys to fill in that time with their own story of what went on. Even if you give the suspect a break for the restroom, record an empty room.

Part Three

Child Sexual Assault Suspect Interrogations

16. Interrogating Child Molesters

Interrogating suspected child sexual abuser will require all the same techniques as discussed in previous chapters, with a few additions. Before you can get confessions from child molesters you have to understand their mind and yours. Not everyone can be good at getting confessions from people who have sexually abused children. Many investigators simply can not get their attitude right to deal with this type of offender. They have an impossible time showing empathy and concern for the suspect. While I understand that, if you are that investigator and cannot get past it, do not go into that room. You will likely be wasting your time and ruining any chance of anyone else getting a confession.

The best investigators in this type of interrogation understand the mind of a child abuser. Whereas I cannot give you a degree in pedophilia psychology, I can give you some really good insight into the mind of a sexual abuser. I spent many years studying this topic and talking with and interrogating child sexual offenders. I made it my priority to get confessions and limit the chance of reoffending. I decided I would do whatever it took to get them either in prison, in counseling, or both and away from children. To date my confession rate for child sexual offenders is around 98%.

Confessions in these cases are vital. A good clean confession will likely ensure a plea and thus further insulate the victim from more distress. If a suspect confesses he or she will often times want to avoid the embarrassment of a court trial. A good confession will most likely convince a defense attorney to recommend a plea. A plea means the victim will not have to go to court and relive the abuse all while looking at their abuser. Often times the abuser is a family member and one the victim loves. This is a situation I want to avoid in as many cases as I can, a good confession helps.

To get confessions from a child sexual abuser you must be able to feign empathy and compassion toward these suspects. You need to understand these offenders have a real compulsion to offend and do not understand why.

17. Pedophilia Psychology

Before you can ever get a confession from a pedophile you must understand them and the way their mind works. There are two types of pedophiles: Regressed and Fixated

Regressed Pedophile (situational)

In this type of pedophile, the psychosexual development of the offender was normal beyond the adolescent stage. This situational offender has been able to maintain a traditional sexual relationship with adults. However, when stresses of life or certain triggers occur, they are more comfortable with children. The offender regresses when feelings of inadequacy intrude.

Fixated Pedophile (preference)

This offender has not experienced a "normal" sex life and likely never been married. The offender's job and/or recreational activities places them in a situation where they must deal with children. This offender did not develop normally through adolescence and likely has had these compulsions toward younger people since early in life.

Pre and Post Pubescent

Both types of pedophiles have a sexual paraphilia toward children. Some may be attracted to prepubescent children (before they have started puberty) or post pubescent children (after puberty has began, generally young teens). The post pubescent pedophile prefers children who have started puberty, around the age of 12 or 13 and will be un-attracted at about the age of 16. These pedophiles want the child to have started the development process of pubic hair and/or breast growth, and have reached a point where they (the child) could receive some physical pleasure from the abuse, such as orgasm. After about the age of 16 the child has developed more adult like features and the attraction is gone. Pre-pubescent offenders are only concerned with their desires and do not care about the child having any physical pleasure.

The following is summary from The DSM-IV-TR

Ephebophilia

Ephebophilia is the primary or exclusive adult sexual interest in mid-to-late adolescents, generally ages 15 to 19. The term was originally used in the late 19th to mid 20th century. It is one of a number of sexual preferences across age groups subsumed under the technical term chronophilia. Ephebophilia strictly denotes the *preference* for mid-to-late adolescent sexual partners, not the mere presence of some level of sexual attraction.

Mid-to-late adolescents usually have physical characteristics near (or, in some cases, identical) to that of fully-grown adults; psychiatrist and sexologist Fred Berlin states that most men can find persons in this age group sexually attractive, but that "of course, that doesn't mean they're going to act on it. Some men who become involved with teenagers may not have a particular disorder. Opportunity and other factors may have contributed to their behaving in the way they do".

Researchers state that hebephilia, erotic interest which centers on young pubescent's, has not come into widespread use, even among professionals who work with sex offenders, and may have been confused with the term ephebophilia, which denotes a preference for older adolescents. It is concluded that "few would want to label erotic interest in late — or even mid — adolescents as a psychopathology, so the term hebephilia may have been ignored along with ephebophilia".

In research environments, specific terms are used for chronophilias: (a form of paraphilia in which an individual experiences sexual attraction limited to individuals of particular age ranges) for instance, ephebophilia to refer to the sexual preference for mid-to-late adolescents, hebephilia to refer to the sexual preference for earlier pubescent individuals, and pedophilia to refer to the sexual preference for prepubescent children.

- However, the term pedophilia is commonly used by the general public to refer to any sexual interest in minors below the legal age of consent, regardless of their level of physical or mental development.

Paraphilia

To understand the mind of any sexual offender (not just child offenders) you must understand paraphilia. Lets first look at the definition.

A paraphilia is a psychosexual disorder in which sexual gratification is obtained through practices or fantasies involving a bizarre, deviant, or highly unusual source of sexual arousal such as an animal or object. **Psychosexual** is; of or relating to, the mental and emotional aspects of sexuality.

In short, paraphilia's are considered to be a component of a person's entire psychological makeup. They cannot be "fixed", but their effects can be suppressed. This should not be looked at as mere preferences. They are seen as being pervasive, affecting all components of a person's lifestyle, thinking and emotional states.

The DSM-IV-TR lists the following paraphilias:

Exhibitionism: the recurrent urge or behavior to expose one's genitals to an unsuspecting person. **Fetishism:** the use of non-sexual or nonliving objects or part of a person's body to gain sexual excitement. Partialism refers to fetishes specifically involving non-sexual parts of the body. **Frotteurism**: the recurrent urges or behavior of touching or rubbing against a non-consenting person. **Masochism**: the recurrent urge or behavior of wanting to be humiliated, beaten, bound, or otherwise made to suffer. **Sadism:** the recurrent urge or behavior involving acts in which the pain or humiliation of the victim is sexually exciting. **Voyeurism**: the recurrent urge or behavior to observe an unsuspecting person who is naked, disrobing or engaging in sexual activities, or may not be sexual in nature at all. **Transvestite fetishism**: a sexual attraction towards the clothing of the opposite gender. **Chronophilias such as Infantophilia**: the sexual attraction to infants; Pedophilia: the sexual attraction to prepubescent children; **Gerontophilia:** the sexual attraction to the elderly

Other paraphilias: this is a grouping of rarer paraphilias including such problems as telephone scatalogia (obscene phone calls), necrophilia (corpses), partualism (exclusive focus on one part of the body), zoophilia (animals), coprophilia (feces), klismaphilia (enemas), (urine) urophilia

<u>Special Note:</u> Homosexuality (gay and lesbianism) was previously listed as a paraphilia in the DSM-I and DSM-II, but this was declassified from both DSM-III and DSM-IV, consistent with the change of attitude among psychiatrists and psychologists. Homosexuality is no longer considered a paraphilia.

So, you have to ask yourself these questions

- Are pedophiles born or are they made?
- What does genetic makeup play in these decisions to offend?
- Why are they attracted to children?
- Could past abuse have caused them to start offending?
- How does this sexual tendency differ or align with homosexuality (minus the crime)?
- Are these offenders better or worse than serial rapist?
- Does the fact the children are involved make it worse? Why?

Offender psychology in summary

As you can see, a child sexual abuser has many reasons why they think the way they think. The most important thing for you to take away from all of that is this: these offenders are hurting children, yes, but why? Understand their desire to do so is compulsive and a part of who they are. The guy that breaks into houses, or steals cars, or kills someone in a bar all had more choices in doing what they did than a child molester. I know they still have a choice to offend or not, but the thief is usually not driven by psychological disorders other than his desire to have what someone else has.

As you read above, homosexuality was only recently taken out of the DSM as a disorder, and not to argue that point, let me say this. If homosexuality was seen as a disorder and has been taken out because it has been determined that it is not a disorder but rather simply who the person is, could pedophilia be seen the same way. In fact, the DSM states that ephebophilia, the attraction to teens, is not classified as pedophilia, which is the definition of attraction to prepubescent children.

When I teach this subject to investigators I ask them to explain to me why they are attracted to their wife or husband. Not the person specifically but the gender. If a heterosexual male, tell me why you are attracted to women, be specific. Why are you attracted to women and not men, give me specific reasons why mentally you are not attracted to men. No one has ever been able to. You cannot explain to me why you are attracted to one gender over another, you just are. You are the way you are, whatever that may be. Child sexual abusers are the same way. They do not know why they feel the way they do and most, if not all, wished they didn't.

The next time you are faced with interrogating a suspect accused of a sexual crime against a child less than 18 years old, remember what you read here. Approach these suspects with the understanding that this is part of their metal makeup and may be derived from a psychological disorder; you will have a better interrogation when you understand this. You will be able to have some empathy and maybe a little compassion. Not that what they did was okay and not criminal, but your goal needs to be getting the confession so that other children will be safer.

18. Pedophile Interrogation

As with all interrogations you must know your case facts and everything you can about the suspect. Use all the same preparation tools discussed in earlier chapters. These cases are more "HE said SHE said" cases than many others. Rarely will you have much, if any, physical evidence. It is the rare case where you have an immediate complaint and physical evidence such as wounds and semen found. Most of the cases are reported weeks, months, and years later. Even if a report comes only hours after the abuse, physical evidence might not exist or has been destroyed.

You must approach these interrogations with the right attitude. Empathy and compassion are key in these cases. The suspect you are dealing with knows the stigma attached to what he is accused of and he will not admit anything to you if he feels you are setting in judgment of him, or her as the case may be.

Establish Credibility

An investigator must establish credibility with the offender by showing that he really understands human sexuality and deviance. A pseudo therapeutic approach, where the investigator communicates with the offender in a nonthreatening and nonjudgmental way, showing understanding and empathy, has a much greater chance of success than aggressive confrontation. None of this will work however, if the investigator does not understand the psychology of offenders.

In a recent study published by the Police Chief Magazine, three key components existed in getting offenders to confess.

Understanding the Psychology of Child Molesters: A Key to Getting Confessions

By Tom O'Connor, Chief of Police, and William Carson, Captain, Maryland Heights, Missouri, Police Department

1. Demonstrate Respect in the Interview

The most consistent reason offered by the offenders for why they confessed their crime was the immediate and constant respect shown them by the interviewer. Respect meant several things to them. In some cases, the interviewer engaged in nonthreatening, nonspecific, non-crime-related conversation. The interviewer clearly demonstrated a psychological understanding of sex offenders and was able to create a feeling that the interviewer, as one offender stated, "cared about my issues and showed real concern for me as a human being."

One told us: "He was the first policeman who ever treated me right. He made me feel like a real person, not a criminal." Another said, "I have been treated like s- by the police all of my life. I didn't think any of them were any good or gave a damn about anybody but themselves. When Detective ____ talked to me, he treated me like a man, not a kid. He was tough but fair, and never once did he ever talk down to me."

2. Develop Rapport

The second significant reason for confessing was the "ease of conversation" and a perception that the interviewer quickly established trust and understanding and could provide them with help. Participants described how they were "short-circuited," expecting a "police bully" and instead finding the opposite and actually liking the interviewer. Conversation was easy; it was not difficult to confess to someone they perceived as a friend.

3. Show Empathy

The third successful interviewing technique acknowledged by the offenders as being "very helpful" to them in deciding whether or not to admit to their crime was showing understanding and empathy. Empathy is the ability of the interviewer to view the world of the sexual offender through the offender's eyes. Empathy is also, in part, an understanding of why the subject is an offender, why his sexual attraction to children exists.

Investigators who communicate that they feel the molester is "repulsive" and cannot easily sit and talk with the offender will not be successful. Many of the molesters interviewed indicated it was obvious what the police really thought of them, making it difficult for them to relate to the interviewer. The molesters reported that they realized within seconds of contact with the police that there would be no real rapport or honest conversation. Their sense of what the interviewer thought of them came through loud and clear with their introductory words, the practiced mechanical delivery of words that oozed incongruity and betrayed inner feelings of disgust. As one said: "If he only knew what I was feeling inside, how sorry I was, it would have been easier for me to talk. He had that look about him; he tried, but I couldn't talk with him." **end of article**

Reason Formulation

As with all other suspects, it is easier sometimes to get an initial admission on your way to the full confession if you can help them establish some reason formulation.

- Blame urges
- Drugs-alcohol
- Their own past abuse
- Blame the victim if you need to

Most suspects in these cases want to talk, you just need to give them a reason to do so. Another area detailed in the above noted article was reasons given by a suspect as to why they confessed. You can use these in your conversation to help them over the edge of deciding to confess. Reasons given for the confession were.

- Desire to prevent the victim from having to publicly identify him in court as a sexual offender.

- Desire to save the victim from being traumatized by the system.

- Because of his love and concern for the victim, desire to spare the victim the negative publicity associated with being a victim of sexual abuse.

- Desire to avoid embarrassing the suspect's family.

- Desire to obtain treatment and learn to control his sexual attraction to children.

- Desire to express remorse for his actions and demonstrate his concern by helping the victims find answers and closure.

- Desire to take responsibility for his actions.

- Disgust with himself.

- Guilt (the internal acknowledgment that one is responsible for one's criminal deeds) greater than shame (the reaction to public knowledge of the crime).

- Belief, based on the rapport between suspect and police interviewer, that now would be the best time for a confession.

- Belief that the police interviewer understood why the suspect was a sexual offender and why he was involved in criminal sexual behavior.
- Belief that the police interviewer understood the suspect's desperate need for acceptance from anyone, children included, as the suspect had always perceived himself as one who is lonely, uncared for by society, unloved by those who should have loved him, and unable to deal with rejection.
- Belief that the suspect was blameless, because the child had initiated the sexual contact.
- Belief that the suspect had demonstrated more concern for the child than the child's own parents.
- Belief that the child was old enough to enjoy the sexual contact.
- Belief that the suspect had never forced the child to do anything.
- Belief that the police interviewer understood that the suspect truly loved and cared for children.
- Belief that the sex act was only a small part of the overall relationship.
- Belief that the police interviewer understood that the child victim really did care for the suspect.
- Religious beliefs about what is right and wrong.

Key Point

Getting a full confession is crucial. There is a difference between an admission and a confession. An admission is a partial acknowledgment of the facts of the crime. A confession contains a description of all the elements of the crime. A good investigator can bring closure to many other crimes by being thorough during the interview process and not being too quick to accept a suspect's assertions that this was his first and only victim.

19. A Final Word

It is my hope that after reading this book you have found new information and strategies to help you get the information and the confession you seek. I understand there are a lot of techniques out there and some major training in this field. Admittedly, this work is probably some hybrid of all you have ever learned as it is for me.

Over my 30 years of law enforcement investigations I have found what works for me, a slight change here, different wording there, it all adds up to fitting everything I have learned into my personality. You will do this too, and that's ok. This book is MY way and albeit a good way, certainty not the only way. Suspects are different and investigators are different.

The key thing to remember from this book is that empathy and rapport goes a lot further than force and intimidation. Further, you must keep in mind that interrogating child sexual assault suspects must be done with a different approach than any other crime and it takes a special investigator to do them right.

Regardless of where you are in your career and however long you've been working in this field, you never stop learning. Spend time reading and taking courses on this subject, especially if you are going to be good at interrogating pedophiles you must learn all you can about how their mind works and what drives the urges they have.

Remember, information is only a question away!

Appendix

Miranda Rights Warning

Before we ask you any questions, you must understand your rights:

- You have the right to remain silent.
- Anything you say can and will be used against you in a court of law
- You have the right to an attorney.
- If you cannot afford an attorney, one will be appointed for you before any questioning if you wish one
- You can decide at any time from this moment on to terminate the interview and exercise these rights. Do you understand each of these rights I have explained to you?

Having these rights in mind, do you wish to talk to us now?

Acknowledgment Statement

I have read, or have read to me, each of my rights, and I fully understand each one and I am willing to answer questions and make a statement at this time. I do not want the advice of an attorney at this time. I understand and know what I am doing . No promises or threats have been made to me

Location Advised	Date Advised	Time Advised	
Print Name	Signature	Date	Time
Investigator Name	Signature	Date	Time

Juvenile Miranda Rights Warning

Before we ask you any questions, you must understand your rights:

- You have the right to remain silent.
- Anything you say can and will be used against you in a court of law
- You have the right to an attorney.
- If you cannot afford an attorney, one will be appointed for you before any questioning if you wish one
- You have the right to talk to your parent(s)/guardian(s) and have them present with you during any questioning
- If you wish to communicate with an attorney, parent or guardian, all reasonable means will be provided to do so.
- You can decide at any time from this moment on to terminate the interview and exercise these rights. Do you understand each of these rights I have explained to you?

Having these rights in mind, do you wish to talk to us now?

Acknowledgment Statement

I have read, or have read to me, each of my rights, and I fully understand each one and I am willing to answer questions and make a statement at this time. I do not want the advice of an attorney at this time. I understand and know what I am doing . No promises or threats have been made to me.

Location Advised	Date Advised	Time Advised	
Print Name	Signature	Date	Time
Investigator Name	Signature	Date	Time

AUTHORIZATION FOR DISCLOSURE OF HEALTH INFORMATION

Authorization for Use/Disclosure of Information: I voluntarily consent to authorize my health care provider ____ (insert name) to use or disclose my health information during the term of this Authorization to the recipient(s) that I have identified below.

Recipient: I authorize my health care information to be released to the following recipient(s):

Agency Name:____

Purpose: I authorize the release of my health information for the following specific purpose: For use in a criminal investigation or inquiry

Information to be disclosed: I authorize the release of the following health information: (check the applicable box below)

- ❑ All of my health information that the provider has in his or her possession, including information relating to any medical history, mental or physical condition and any treatment received by me.[1]
- ❑ Only the following records or types of health information: ____.

Term: I understand that this Authorization will remain in effect:

- ❑ From the date of this Authorization until the _____ day of ________, 20___.
- ❑ Until the Provider fulfills this request.
- ❑ Until the following event occurs:____

______________________	______________________	______________________
Signature	Date	Signature of Witness

If Individual is unable to sign this Authorization, please complete the information below:

Name of Guardian/ Representative	Legal Relationship	Date	Witness

____

Resources

We get Confessions ISBN: 0-9647448-0-5 *By: Lieut. Albery Joseph Jr.*
Copyright 1995

Police Chief Magazine
Article February 2016
Understanding the Psychology of Child Molesters: A Key to Getting Confessions
By Tom O'Connor, Chief of Police, and William Carson, Captain, Maryland Heights, Missouri, Police Department

DSM-IV-TR
Diagnostic and Statistical Manual of Mental Disorders
American Psychiatric Association

THE FORGOTTEN AREA CANVASS
By Sgt. (Ret.) Tony Monheim, MS
Reprinted from Law and Order Magazine

About the Author

Darren Dake is an ABMDI accredited medicolegal death investigator and an ACFEI certified criminal investigator working with Crawford County Missouri, an author, conference speaker, trainer, and podcast-media producer. He has a tri-balanced background in law enforcement investigations, corporate leadership, and Christian ministry.

Darren is a certified teaching instructor and criminal investigator with over 30 years' experience in the field of law enforcement and death investigations. He holds certification as an instructor for the American College of Forensic Examiners, Missouri Department of Public Safety, the Missouri Sheriff's Association, and the Law Enforcement Training Institute - (Missouri University Columbia). Darren is also the lead instructor and facilitator for the Death Investigation Training Academy™, and hosts its online podcast-media program for death investigators.

To contact the author or to learn more about training opportunities in your area through the Death Investigation Training Academy and other books written by Darren - go to:

ditacademy.org

Made in the USA
Middletown, DE
21 November 2017